Black Women Love

A Tribute To Love From The Unique Perspective Of Black Women

By
Kenneth Wilson

Co-authored by Phenomenal Women of Power

2023

A TRIBUTE TO LOVE FROM
THE UNIQUE PERSPECTIVE
OF BLACK WOMEN

BLACK WOMEN

LOVE

KENNETH WILSON
&
14 PHENOMENAL WOMEN OF POWER

Copyright © 2023 by Kenneth Wilson

All rights reserved. This book or any portion thereof may not be reproduced or used in any manner whatsoever without the express written permission of the publisher except for the use of brief quotations in a book review or scholarly journal.

First Printing: 2023

ISBN: 979-8-3783043-0-1

Ordering Information:

Special discounts are available on quantity purchases by corporations, associations, educators, and others. For details, contact the publisher at the email listed below.

U.S. trade bookstores and wholesalers:
Please contact kennywilson65@gmail.com

DEDICATION

I dedicate this book to the most important women in my life. My mother Sandra Ann Robinson. My wife Leanne Wilson. My daughters Lilianna, Alexandra, and Annette Wilson. I draw my strength and motivation from you all. Thank you for helping me become the man I am today. I love you.

PREFACE

At a young age, I was able to experience and understand the unique power and perspective of black women. The power that comes from generations of resilience and overcoming unimaginable obstacles. Black women have endured the entire spectrum of humanity. They have been treated as less than human. They have also been admired for their unrivaled beauty, grace, and strength. Those experiences have given black women a unique wisdom. We need black women to balance and complete our culture. To put it simply, black men and black women need each other. We must work together in understanding and cooperation, to continue to move our culture forward in a positive direction.

This understanding must include black women sharing their thoughts and perspectives. I have taken a responsibility to provide platforms and opportunities for us to share. For me this journey first began with the creation of Black Men Love in 2022. That book allowed fourteen black men to share their thoughts, experiences, and stories around the concept of love. The book was a success, becoming a bestseller. Even while writing Black Men Love, I knew the conversations could not stop there. Black Women must also be allowed the same opportunity to share. Black Women Love is the continuation of my vision to provide black women those opportunities. Now fourteen black women of all ages and backgrounds have come together to express their thoughts on love.

Love has many definitions, depending on the person's experiences and interpretations. Black Women Love is a true tribute to the layered and multifaceted concept of love. This book is not limited to discussing physical relationships or the opposite sex. These authors have explored their hearts to share what love means to them.

TABLE OF CONTENTS

DEDICATION	iv
PREFACE	v
LIST OF AUTHORS IN CHAPTER ORDER	1
LOVE REDEFINED	2
I CHOOSE ME	12
UNCONDITIONAL FELINE LOVE	20
INSPIRATION IS LOVE	24
NO EXPECTATIONS. NO ATTACHMENTS	30
DIRECT WITH RESPECT & RESPECTED DUE TO DIRECTNESS	38
THE LOVE FOR OUR BLACK CHILDREN	46
UNVEILING LOVE'S TRUE IDENTITY	56
AS YOURSELF	62
MY FIRST LOVE	72
OH, TO BE BOUNDLESS	76
THAT "AS IS" LOVE	86
THE LOVE EXPERIENCE	96
I HATE THAT I LOVE YOU	102
ABOUT THE LEAD AUTHOR	112
PICK UP THESE OTHER TITLES BY KENNETH WILSON	114
WORK WITH KENNETH	115

LIST OF AUTHORS IN CHAPTER ORDER

1. Ashley Ewell
2. Ashlin Price
3. Brianna Marcelline
4. Cynveda Amelia R.
5. Danielle Frisby
6. Empress Bianca
7. Kennesha Wilson
8. **MsVibrations**
9. NaTasha Tierra
10. Robyn Christian
11. Samantha Hutchison
12. Shaniece Watkins
13. Toyre Davis
14. Yendi Jones

LOVE REDEFINED

Ashley Ewell

Love, to me, does not have only one clear cut meaning, it has several. Love, to me, is friendship, security, trust, loyalty, honesty, transparency, and so much more. However, I did not always think of love in this way. As a little girl, I only thought of love as being just a feeling. I thought of the moment when a woman walks down the aisle in a beautiful white dress towards her husband. I thought of it being as simple as my mom and dad. However, in time, my concept of love changed. It took a few failed attempts at romantic relationships before I realized that love is more than that. I had to learn that before you can truly give any of those components of love to anyone else you have to give them to yourself. As a teenager growing up, there was a time that I struggled and had low self-esteem. I was my own worst critic and failed to see the beauty in who I was. It took a lot of work to get myself to where I am today. I had to boost my self-confidence and tell myself that I was beautiful, despite the flaws I internalized. I had to love myself to know how I wanted to be loved and truly believe that I deserved to be loved in that exact way. It took a lot of self-reflection, talking to my mom, confiding in my sister, and endless diary entries before I was at a better place mentally and emotionally. Once I was able to successfully do that, it was put to the test in my early twenties when I first began dating.

Through different dating experiences, I quickly learned the type of man I did and didn't want in my life. It wasn't until after my first real heartbreak that I decided to take time to myself and go back to working on self-improvement. This meant taking a break from entertaining people and choosing to focus solely on myself. It wasn't the easiest thing to do. In the beginning I felt the societal pressure to meet someone, get married by thirty, then start a family. I felt that pressure even more because I was off to a late start. I didn't begin dating until I was in my twenties.

I eventually realized that putting myself on such a timeframe was ridiculous and unhealthy. Placing that type of pressure on myself would only lead me to tolerating treatment from a person that I normally wouldn't accept, because I felt that I was running out of time. The truth is that finding love and starting a family will come in Gods timing, whether it comes at twenty-eight or at thirty-four. When it's supposed to happen, it will happen. Until then, I choose to live my life on my terms, being happy and having fun. I also learned that it is also important to speak up and express myself. It's easier to think, "He should already know what I want."

That's the furthest thing from the truth. No one can read another person's mind. If I don't express what I want and need, how will the other person truly be able to try and meet those needs. Realizing all of this was truly a process and sometimes took more periods of trial and error. Once I did, everything began to slowly fall into place.

For about a year and a half I was single. When I say single, I mean completely single. During this time, I dated myself and learned to love myself more. Of course, I met people here and there, but in the end, it was still Ashley party of One. The difference this time around was that I was finally able to accept and be okay with that. I decided that when I started to date again that I would date intentionally. I would not settle for less than what I wanted. If I chose to move forward with a relationship, the person had to desire the same result as me. This meant having similar values, beliefs, and eventually wanting to be married and start a family. A man who would actively and intently pursue me. Thankfully, I was blessed to grow up in a household where I saw first-hand what real love looks like in a marriage. A God-fearing marriage.

I also saw the obstacles that can come up in a marriage as well. My mom is the most loving, selfless, determined, supportive woman to her children and my dad. She showed me how I hoped to be as a wife and mother. My dad is equally loving, selfless, and supportive. He is still the hardest working man I know. No matter what it took, he made sure to take care of us, even if it meant him working jobs he didn't enjoy. Watching him, showed me the type of man I hoped to marry one day. During that specific time when I was single, I wasn't looking to meet that "type of man". I started feeling like that man might not exist. If he did, he was already snatched up, which was more of a reason that I needed to focus on myself.

They say you tend to meet the love of your life when you're not looking. Little did I know, I would meet my person at the new job I started in 2019. I know you're thinking, "Girl you're crazy, office relationships are a red flag. They never work."

The same thoughts were in my mind in the very beginning until I really started to get to know my fiancé, Alonzo. I quickly learned that he wasn't the type of guy that people think of when they think office romance. I can't really explain it, something drew us to each other. In the very beginning of us dating, we had several conversations regarding intentionally dating each other to see if we both wanted the same things. We did. We even took a quiz to learn what each other's love languages are and made attempts to show them. I knew that though we both wanted the same thing, it was important that we built a friendship first. This has always been what I felt was the foundation of a healthy relationship.

Forming a friendship with him came naturally, it was almost as if I knew him my whole life. We enjoyed each other's company and always had fun together. To be honest, I was nervous at first, I thought that he might be too good to be true. Alonzo was doing things that I always wanted to see from a man who said that he wanted to be with me. He would surprise me with flowers, take me on fun dates, check on me, listen to me, support me etc. Everything he said he was going to do, he showed with his actions not just his words. I already knew I really liked him. Like soon turned into love. This wasn't because of the nice things that he would get me or do for me, it was because of who he was as a person and who I was when I was with him. At his core I could see that he was genuinely a good person with a big heart. As a bonus, I saw that he was even better as a father to his son. Things were simple when I was with him. Every time I was around him it felt like home. After dating for six months, he asked me to be his girlfriend and the rest was history.

We took the time to get to know each other and learn how to love each other. As I referenced before, knowing each other's love languages was one of our first steps. It helped that some of our top love languages were very similar. Words of affirmation, acts of service, and quality time were high on both of our lists. It wasn't, and still isn't a difficult task to show him these love languages. I love affirming Alonzo. Whether I'm telling him how proud I am of him, or something as simple as telling him how handsome he is, or how nicely he's dressed. Acts of service simply means showing up for him how I would want him to show up for me. This can be running an errand for him, taking care of him when he's sick, or simply making his favorite dish after a long stressful day. Then there's quality time, which means intently setting aside time to spend with him, even it's simply relaxing in the house while eating snacks and watching movies.

I show and express my love to him the best way I know how. Of course, if there are things we hoped to see more of, we express that to each other. That seemed to be one of the easier parts of our relationship. The hardest part of our relationship however wasn't too far behind.

I always heard that the first six months is usually the honeymoon period of a relationship, boy was that the truth. After the initial period, things did get rocky and we started facing some obstacles. The biggest obstacle for us was our communication. Part of learning to love each other is also learning how to communicate. We struggled with knowing how we should talk to each other, especially when things were heated. Of course, there were arguments and times things seemed hard. This was because we didn't take the time to learn how to communicate effectively. After an argument it was easy to "sweep the argument under the rug". Sitting down to have the conversation and figure out a resolution was the hard part. We would sweep and sweep, until the pile became too high, which only led to bigger blow ups.

We didn't learn our lesson the first few times so it would happen repeatedly until we both grew tired. Eventually, we gave each other some space. We later had a conversation and decided that there needed to be a solution to this. He had to be honest about his triggers and I had to be honest about mine. He had to realize what he needed to improve on, and I did as well. For me, I had to learn that I didn't need to have a comment for everything and that I must choose my battles wisely. I also learned not to be so easily offended and learn the best way to approach Alonzo when expressing myself based on his triggers. This wasn't an easy thing to do and honestly something I am still working on.

For us, completely giving up on each other was not an option. Things would be different if either of us no longer wanted to put in the effort. However, we were both willing to work on things and put in equal effort to make our relationship better. Though it can hurt, the hard conversations are necessary. We are still learning to do that. Sometimes we do great at it and other times we don't. We never look for perfection in each other because perfection isn't real, everyone has something they can improve on. What it always boils down to for us is that underneath all those feelings of love, we really are best friends. No matter how many times I may get on his nerves, he may get on mine, or we disagree, that fact never changes. He's still the first person I want to wake up to see, tell my exciting news, and have fun with. Our relationship may not be everyone's cup of tea and that's okay because it's ours and ours alone. There will always be obstacles that will come up, but we know, that if we keep God first and tackle things together, we will be just fine. Three years and a baby later, I couldn't love Alonzo more or be more excited to see what life holds for our relationship. Now that I'm thirty, I've realized that my concept of love has not changed. Instead, I understand love more and know how to show it better. Although certain aspects of my life are not exactly where I would like for them to be, they're exactly where they should be. I can proudly say that after being unapologetically true to myself, loving me, trusting my journey, and letting love find me, it is now Ashley Party of Four.

ABOUT THE AUTHOR:

Social Media:
IG @simply_ashx3
FB @ashley.ewell.9
Email ash.ewell92@gmail.com

Ashley Ewell, born and raised in the Bronx, NY, is a passionate program coordinator who has been in the health and human services field for over seven years. After her family moved to Maryland, when she was seventeen years old, her love for the field of health and human services began. She attended the University of Maryland Eastern Shore where she graduated with her B.S. in Rehabilitation Services. Ashley used this degree to work in the field of helping individuals with developmental disabilities. Once she completed her degree, she was able to do just that, by getting her first job working at a school in D.C. that served children with intellectual disabilities. After a few years of being employed at different companies, she made the choice to go back to school to get her Masters in Healthcare Administration. She went to the University of Maryland University College and graduated with a 3.8 G.P.A. Using this degree Ashley moved up in her field to become a liaison for coordinators for the State of Maryland. Recently, Ashley and her sister started a jewelry business called Majestic Jewels in memory of their grandmother and great grandmother who had recently passed. This online boutique sells all things jewelry and accessories, such as earrings, necklaces, sunglasses and, more. Although she is proud of her business, her greatest accomplishment was having her son in May 2022. During her free time, she enjoys being a mom, spending time with her fiancé, family and friends as well as selling jewelry.

I CHOOSE ME

Ashlin Price

When I hear the word LOVE, it is usually attached and compared to the questions or statements, "Do you have children? Are you married? Where is your man? Do you want to be married? You are getting too old to have kids. Get rid of that man he is no good for you. What are you waiting for? Why is it taking so long?"

And to me it usually sounds like, "You're not good enough. Why are you single? A woman needs a man. You're not valuable without children. You can't even keep a man. Why are you so picky? You're not enough."

My question then becomes, "Why does love have to be attached and based on the measurement of someone or something else capacity?"

Hardly anyone ever says, "How are you feeling in this journey of singleness? What are you learning about yourself? You are right where you need to be. Waiting has purpose and time never lacks. What do you need to fulfill yourself in this space?"

Why can't I just love me and enjoy this space I'm in? No one knows what it took for me to get to this place of freedom, this place of joy, of peace, and of recognition. No one knows how I communicate love and why I love the way that I do. How can you tell me what love is supposed to look like in my life?

It was when I decided to compromise and sacrifice myself when I really found love within me. It was when I felt like I loved him more than I considered myself. It was when I went into a depression, and I knew that I needed to consider myself to smile again. It was when I changed the ending of the relationship and parted ways. I've never loved anyone the I way loved him, and I knew I needed to love myself just a little more than I loved the situation. It was when I had the hard conversations with myself and with GOD about what His purpose was for my life. I began to understand the desires and visions He has for my life. I knew that solely surrendering the process would be a challenge, but I was willing to surrender for glory.

My parents weren't married so I've never really seen an immediate perspective of healthy love and that was a challenge for me. I have seen long term relationships, I have seen "shacking up", and I have seen long term friendship. Although marriage was not something I had seen in my household, I have witnessed amazing and great marriages. I knew they existed, and I knew I was able to have the same thing because I was able to see it and had a desire for it.

The obstacles and challenges I encountered had nothing to do with "him" but had more to do with me. I didn't see value within myself. I didn't see my worth. I didn't see that I was compromising myself and putting myself on the back burner to ensure that it would work. For me to love someone, I had to make sure that I genuinely loved every aspect of me, the good, the bad, and the indifferent. I had to fall in love with all the things I didn't like. I had to fall in love with the things that I did like. I had to fall in love with all the things that scared me and pushed me out of my own way. Once I was able to see me how God sees me, to really understand how God wants to nurture and protect me, I began to understand how sincere and precious I was to the earth. This reminds me of the infamous question that everyone wants to know, "What is your love language?"

Out of the five-love languages my top two are words of affirmation and acts of service. In finding myself I literally had to affirm my value by speaking life into me. I felt like I had to qualify myself again to be shared, to be loved, to be cared for, given compliments, and to share a space. I felt like I had to earn love, earn the right to be seen, and earn the privilege of being heard. I was tired of being a secret, tired of my time being shared, and tired of not having clarity. I would listen to positive affirmations daily, write affirmations on sticky notes, write in my journal, and speak it out loud to myself every day. To love myself I had to let him go. I had to sacrifice myself and compromise my happiness to make room for FAITH, clarity, peace, joy, abundance, prosperity, and elevation. I had to make room for ME, for me to live and consider myself. I had to let go of depression, feelings of anxiety, and overthinking. I had to ask God for healing, to take the pain away and just allow me to be whole again, but I felt broken in that space of transition.

The moment I realized I loved myself more than the situation was when I had to inflict pain upon myself. I knew greater was coming and I had to choose me. The hardest thing I've ever had to do in this thing called Love is to choose Me. Choose me in the confusion. Choose me when I was overwhelmed. Choose me through anxiety and depression. Choose me when I didn't want to be chosen and choose me when I did want to be chosen. Choose me when I didn't feel valuable. I needed to take myself off reserve and be on the show case for me. I needed to date me, hangout with me, heal me, pamper me, sing sweet songs to me, send myself flowers, and just really surrender to the higher power. I needed myself to know that I am worthy, I am deserving, I am valuable, I am worth the investment, and I am enough. There were many times when I didn't feel like any of those things.

I want a love that is ever lasting, accountable, and stern yet firm. I want a love that speaks life, liberation, and peace to me, yet can also tell me when I'm acting like a brat and being stubborn. I grew up without my mother and my father in the household. I lived with my grandmother until she passed away when I was eight years old then I moved in with my aunt who I call "mom". The most consistent man I've seen in my life was my brother. My brother bought me things for Christmas. He bought me my first car. He drove me to college and helped me move into my dorm. He paid for all the maintenance on my car. He gave my mother money for groceries.

He would take out the trash and just make sure things around the house were taken care of. That was my first impression of love from a man. My brother was not perfect. He had lots of flaws, but I knew that when I needed something he would be there. When I became an adult, I started building a relationship with my father. I did my best to put all my biases and judgements aside and just love my father even though I was hurting. I use these two examples as reference to say that my perspectives of love from men vary. I didn't live with my father, so my first love wasn't my father, but it was seeing other girls with their fathers, seeing how other men treated their women and their daughters. I knew that love was real. I knew that before I could ever encounter any of that, I needed to heal from my personal traumas, my past perspectives, and beliefs about love and how to be loved.

Me versus me is essentially about creating a space for myself to be vulnerable, listening to what I want and need in my life. It's about challenging my insecurities, facing my fears, being obedient, listening to my inner voice, and creating a space for me to fall in love. Falling in love with me is about truly taking the time out to teach me, to figure out what I like and dislike, it's about being bold with what I want and asking for what I need. It's not about making excuses for my standards or boundaries. Realizing that I don't have to feel bad when someone doesn't meet them. It's about always making myself a priority. It's about being selfish with me, my time, and my energy. Being in a posture to tell people that this space in my life is "invitation only". I knew that I was falling in love with ME when I chose myself. God was making changes, shifting things around and making myself a priority when I learned to love ME. God allowed me to heal my wounds by creating a space of patience, intimacy, vulnerability, and surrender. I knew love was the best gift I could give to myself when growing and maturing so I could genuinely love others. Black Women love isn't just about loving others but about showing up for yourself so you can show up for others in a healthy manner.

ABOUT THE AUTHOR:

Social Media:

IG @the_money_socialworker

FB @ashlin.price

Email ashlin.price@gmail.com

Ashlin Price is a sought-after speaker and financial literacy consultant who specializes in providing financial literacy, addressing behaviors related to finances, and professional development. She is the owner of Financial Freedom Enterprises, LLC, a financial consultant company that provides services to communities and organizations in need of financial education and strategic planning to improve their personal and professional finances.

Ashlin is a Licensed Master Social Worker (LMSW) in Maryland, a Certified Associate Counselor-Alcohol and Drug, with experience in working with juvenile justice, family investment, addictions, child welfare and mental/behavioral health. Ashlin is a Board Approved Supervisor Certified Associate Counselor-Alcohol and Drug. She is also a Certified Prepare and Enrich Marriage Facilitator where she works with couples to foster healthy relationships, understand family dynamics of communication, conflict resolution, financial literacy, and encourage open communication. She has been a guest and featured on various media platforms to discuss personal and financial health and wellness.

Ashlin possesses a master's degree in Social Work from the University of Maryland Baltimore and a bachelor's degree in

Rehabilitation Services from University of Maryland Eastern Shore. She is an active board member for Cheer Up Wellness and TaylorsMOM, two non-profit organizations in Maryland. Ashlin resides in Maryland and serves her community proudly.

UNCONDITIONAL FELINE LOVE

Brianna Marcelline

I feel as though experiencing true, unconditional love is a scarce feeling or experience. When it is experienced, it's a beautiful eye-opening thing. Now you might think you'd experience this from a loved one or even your seed, but it stretches beyond that to me. I experience unconditional love from my feline, my entire heart, and best friend, Mango.

Mango is a five-year-old cat I got on my fourteenth birthday that has not left my side since his rescue. We named the little guy Mango because he's a very round chunky boy with long orange hair. It was genuinely a love at first sight connection. I could've chosen any cat in that shelter but something about Mango stood out. We clicked instantly with our eyes when I saw him sad and alone in that tiny shelter cage. It was a sign.

Cats usually take a few weeks to adjust to a new home. Not me and Mango. As soon as I took Mango out his box the day of adoption he crawled into my arms, ignoring everything he'd been through. He sensed that he was safe with me. He could tell I had nothing to provide him other than unconditional love. Since that day, I don't think I've experienced anyone more excited for me to come home from work. I share my food, bed, and emotions with him. I even take him on walks with his cute little harness. He sits there and listens with no back talk.

But other than the cute little activities we do, it took a lot of patience from both of us to mature as we were very young when we met. Believe it or not, Mango didn't listen, and neither did I. Mango had no patience and if he wanted something he wanted it right then and there. That's a big request from a little man with no thumbs. I learned to communicate with gentle parenting as a young cat mom. he would rip up our couch or wipe his butt on our rug which was a huge learning curve. He had to learn that I'm not a cat like him and his playful strikes of terror from his sharp minuscule claws did hurt me. Sometimes I would have to remind myself he's a cat, even though I cared for him like a child. There were nights that I would cry and stress about him when he would sneak past me out the door and be gone for hours. Even though he would always come back, something about knowing I couldn't constantly keep him safe in my arms killed me.

I could keep going on forever about how much I love this little guy and he loves me. All the things we've experienced and been through, but you will never know the absolute love and appreciation a rescued animal will have for its owner until you experience it. It's a beautiful thing. Let me rephrase that, I am not his owner. I am his best friend, and he is mine. I will always give him my unconditional love until I cannot anymore.

ABOUT THE AUTHOR:

Social Media:

IG @imybri

Email brimarc03@gmail.com

Brianna Marcelline is a high school graduate from Montgomery County, Maryland. She currently resides in Anne Arundel County.

Brianna will be attending Anne Arundel County Community College for her first two years. We will see where her passion takes her.

Brianna loves anything that has to do with art, music, or anything pertaining to individuality. She always encourages people to be themselves. Brianna is a big nerd and can talk your head off about video games, anime, or anything of that sort. She streams on Twitch and will kick your butt in chess. She has a deep love for any form of animal, including reptiles, amphibians, mammals, you name it, she's fascinated. This is where her love for her feline Mango stems and will always grow with every day spent with him.

INSPIRATION IS LOVE

Cynveda Amelia R.

At the age of eight, I realized that taking pictures was my passion. One day in school, my class was given a writing assignment to talk about their biggest inspirations. I wrote about my mom because she does everything she says she's going to do and makes her dreams come to life, one step at a time. Most people would not think too much of it, but I was able to witness it firsthand. Sometimes I was a part of the steps that lead to an accomplished goal. Living with your biggest inspiration is powerful. In my case, it was love.

Taking pictures of nature and my beloved cat, Owen, made me feel happy. It gave me hope for the future and so much inspiration on what the future could hold, especially after seeing my mom chase her dreams. Inspiration also came after seeing other young children practice and pursue passions of their own. Summer Pop Up Shopping with my mom and little brother is an annual family tradition that we created and do every weekend of the Summer. If my mom wasn't a pop-up shop employee, she was a customer, and sometimes both. These events opened my eyes to local kid-preneurs (Child Entrepreneurs) I found it fascinating that a child could have their own business and still offer quality. With permission from my mom, I started a public social media page to share my iPhone photos with the world. It wasn't much to share, but it was a start. It's one thing to have family and friends tell you that you take great pictures, but it's another for the world to validate it. The likes and comments received from strangers, professional photographers and even The Oldest Saloon in Washington, DC, Old Ebbitt Grill, inspired me to keep going with this photography journey.

One day I asked my mom if I could take this passion to the next level. The goal was to challenge myself to become so good at taking pictures, that people would want to pay for them. So as my mother transitioned from private event planning to public event planning, Quality Pop Up & Party – Unique Events was born. Quality Pop Up & Party – Unique Events is a series of events created by my mom, customized for those who admire quality over quantity. I have been to enough pop up shops with my mom to know that every pop up shop is not coordinated the same. It was sad to see that many event hosts were clearly just in it for the money and nothing more. So Quality Pop Up & Party – Unique Events was going to change the standard to local pop up shopping events and I wanted to be a part of that. I was given the opportunity to be the exclusive event photographer. This was a huge deal and a lot of pressure for an 11-year-old. To be the sole person responsible for capturing the event pictures was the best thing ever, like a dream come true. I had finally got my shot to be taken seriously as an inspiring photographer. The best part is that I would get paid if done well.

The very first Quality Pop Up & Party – Unique Event, held on June 6, 2021, was my very first paid gig as an event photographer. It was successful, and more fuel added to the tank of inspiration. I, along with so many others, was ready for the next Quality Pop Up & Party - Unique Event to happen as soon as possible! On top of that, I couldn't wait to share my pictures on my new social media page. The recognition and pictures had made its way around to local entrepreneurs. They also wanted to hire me to capture their events on camera. My mom told me that if I was going to make a business out of photography, I would need a plan to provide structure, organization, and a path for success. This is how my business, Captured by Cynveda, was born. My mom coached me on business so much that I had started to doubt and regret getting involved, but I knew that if I really wanted this, it wouldn't come easy. Especially after seeing the different routes my mom had to sometimes take to bring her dreams to life.

The coaching began, the practice continued and before I knew it, I was working gigs, capturing pictures on my iPhone. I wasn't concerned about not having an actual camera, but I knew "real" photographers did and wanted to eventually be seen as one. I worked 6 events and donated photography services multiple times in the year 2021. For me, that was a great first year of business. That Christmas, I received a Christmas tree ornament in the shape of a camera dated 2021. Just another piece of inspirational love from the one who inspired me the most. The next year, I received my very first camera, gifted by another inspirational public figure and mentor of my mom. I knew that the process of editing would be a new learning curve, so I started to take raw pictures and got to know the functions of my new camera. I studied many days and countless hours to learn the camera, and the functions I had never heard of. Thankfully, my iPhone was still around because YouTube and Google can be powerful when used correctly. Although I knew nothing about editing, local Entrepreneurs still wanted to book me for their events and pay for raw photos. In the world of photography, that's pretty wild, but yet again it was another piece of inspirational love. The fact that I (or maybe my affordable prices) was liked so much that people were willing to pay for raw pictures was almost unheard of.

Now, I am almost 13 years old and extremely grateful to have found and pursued something I love. The next goal is to learn the in's and outs of photoshop while finding a local professional photographer who has time to mentor the youth. I absolutely love this talent, business and every bit of inspiration I receive to keep going. -Cynveda Amelia

ABOUT THE AUTHOR:

Social Media:

IG @cynveda

Email capturedbycynveda@gmail.com

Cynveda Amelia is a Child-Entrepreneur who provides the DMV area affordable, quality photography for public and special events.

www.empressbianca.com/cynveda

NO EXPECTATIONS. NO ATTACHMENTS

Danielle Frisby

No Expectations. No Attachments.

That's really how I feel.

It's a decision I made a few months ago and now I affectionately think of these statements as...

My Love Goals...

My Beliefs "To-Be"...

My Prayers after Continuous Clarity...

It's what I'm currently exploring about the Practice of Love.

I desire to Love without expectation in the hopes that I am able to experience moments of peace that are uninterrupted, without apology, and/ or miscommunication.

I desire to Love without attachment in the hopes that I am able to experience moments of closeness absent of traditional ties, bonds, and boundaries.

I view the practice of Love as a lifelong discipline that requires expert-level attention and commitment beyond measure.

I operate from the understanding that Love is limitless and Love will not wait.

I believe that Love knows no time and does not need an invitation. Love is a constant and our universal birthright.

My desire is **"Not to expect.."**
My request is **"Not to attach…"**
My only commitments are to **"Experience and Explore"**

Period.

So No Expectations.

Love is like a train, it is unstoppable. You either catch it or get hit by it.

Because Love is going to happen no matter what and Love cannot be destroyed, we must assume responsibility for its power and proceed with caution.

So No Expectations. It's how we stay safe.

Train tracks…

I believe relationships are more about patterns than people.
Familiar roads and popular routes tend to be sprinkled with regret when we allow unaddressed behaviors and habits to lead the Love journey.

It is because of this that I desire a very specific experience that is powered by honesty and transparent collaboration.

Long story short…I believe that Love is a choice… Love is an action…Love is a responsibility.

As humans, we have become expectant and attached to a way of looking at the world that conflicts with who we naturally are - **Everything has become more important than Love.**

They say…
True love allegedly does not exist
Real love is hard to find and
Fake love makes the most sense

What we continue to fail to realize is that Love is our ultimate reality and our purpose on earth. To be consciously aware of Love and to experience it with others is the meaning of life.

Because Love is like the rain..and the storms are inevitable…
I believe there is no need to *"expect from"* or *"attach to"* other humans as Love in its most natural form is effortless and does not require force. Love is also absent from confusion.

So No Attachments.

I'm saddened by the fact that our children are making masterpieces out of the messes that we have left them. We have allowed them to walk proudly in the painful pathways that we planted for them because we continue to neglect our human nature. We are operating outside of the true definition of love… God is love.
God is love.

Love is not Love. God is Love - and from there Love can be all things.

Keeping Love rooted in God allows it to be purpose-driven and properly attached to people, places, and things. This belief system creates safety and security that allows the limits and bounds of Love to be positioned for shared harmony and continuous growth.

Love is unstoppable and cannot fail. Just like God. **God is Love.**

My belief about Purpose-Driven Love is that it allows you to go past the *"Preliminary Patience Period"*. During this time

- You know that you are supposed to wait on Love
- You know that you are not supposed to rush with Love
- You know that you need to take your time in Love

But for what...why...and for who? These are the open-ended questions that can only truly be answered with purpose-driven responses that allow you to move through the levels of Love that you have been assigned to complete.

You cannot control how you feel...until you can control how you feel...and once you decide to be in control or regain it, you then can go back to the responsibility and ownership that we must assume while operating in and out of Love.

For me deciding on the "purpose of partnership" has drawn me to two specific questions...

"Do I want to have a partner to do nothing with...free time, fun, a love story that clocks in when, when the work clocks out? Or would I like to have a partner that I can't do anything without...every decision, every detail, each step of my dreams?"

No matter the answer or if I ultimately decide that I desire both, my prayer is that we all return to a place of Love so we can all experience all that has been made possible for us. God is Love.

A Simple Prayer before we depart…

I pray that you forget all that you have been taught that goes against the Love that you are made of.

I pray that you remember and/or accept now that you were made in Love and you should be allowed to experience and express it.

I pray for permission and release to be granted for you as you decide to accept the responsibility to remain in and of Love as our Creator has called you to.

And if we can agree that you deserve this moment…and if we can also agree that the Love that you desire is the Love that you already have within you…

Then we both can accept and pray into the private moment that we are sharing within this public book that is only designed for you … And with that, I pray that you continue to Love and consider exploring it without expectations and/or attachments.

Amen.

ABOUT THE AUTHOR:

Social Media:

IG @thatgrlelle

Email hello@unboxingchange.com

Danielle Alease Frisby is an experienced Social Impact Entrepreneur. Her business, Unboxing Change, is an Internship Preparation and Management Organization that trains students Pre-Kindergarten through College to create community impact events and programs centered around Education, Activism, and Entrepreneurship. Student planners are trained to use impact events as tools for business development with a strategic focus on hospitality, sales, and service. Since 2019, UnBoxing Change has worked with student planners and partners to create community brainstorms and events that strengthen neighborhoods, places of worship, and schools. Danielle is a complete believer in holistic healing and planning, her passion for community is deeply rooted in the balance and rhythm of Life, Work, and Love. She works with entrepreneurial children and families to convert their visions for community change into Youth-Driven Volunteer Forces, powered by action steps that remove obstacles and barriers from any project. Learn more at www.unboxingchange.com

DIRECT WITH RESPECT & RESPECTED DUE TO DIRECTNESS

Empress Bianca

Let me tell you something…
First off, Hello.

When loving me, you must know that you're God's Child. Period. I could never subscribe to ordinary, so of course my love matches the energy.

As a young child, there was much ignorance and confusion about my mental health status. Sometimes, when you don't know better, you can't help your children. However, overcoming with awareness, private practice, and supreme focus as a young adult allowed me to have the refreshing quality of life that one could truly ask for. In other words, you can be crazy and choose not to be crazy…Haha!

Love gets really complicated when you've got some mental issues going on, but the best part is, that self-awareness is key. Everything that comes afterwards is what allows the key to work. I learned myself and learned to love myself at the root of self-awareness. You've got to start somewhere and when you do it's going to feel like an elevator ride to the next level. I love positive growth, for myself and others, which is why I'm so grateful and honored to share this experience with a group of phenomenal women. I am the most enthusiastic on the inside and genuinely humbled at the surface.

Thank you so much.

Please Enjoy!

- Empress Bianca

CRAZY IN LOVE
(Uh oh.. Uh oh..)

To be crazy in love with anyone, for me, is to be misunderstood. Personally, my growth comes with logic and to properly love anyone, I had to first learn to love myself. Being misunderstood by many is something I'm used to. I just learned how to bring the good out of the bad. Growing up mentally ill isn't fun, but learning yourself and learning to love yourself restores a power and creates an endless list of self-breakthroughs. Taking the time to figure out why I behaved in such ways that came off as "sensitive" or "crazy" to others was where I started. I asked myself, "Why do you react the way you do?" "What causes these feelings to resort to such angry outbursts?" The journey is always amazing to look back on, because now-a-days the questions I ask myself are elevated, like myself. "Why would I consume my time with someone on a personal level if our level of passion and/or interest doesn't match?" "Is this healthy?"

It was only when I took the time to address myself, with the flaws included, that self-growth was truly planted. As we all know, once you plant your seed, it's destined to sprout with a little tender loving care. I believe in mental health professionals and seeked a few for guidance at different stages of my life. Their professional perspectives helped me to better understand where I was and where I'm going on a level in which, only a professional can articulate. If you're ever stuck in a mental rut, try talking it out and tapping into yourself deeper with a professional.

Come to find out, I'm just extremely passionate. Not just about work, goals, family or continuing education, but everything I give my time to. Not only is the passion extreme, but the personality itself is too. In the mental health community, it's taboo to speak about your personal diagnoses. I am taboo at it's finest. I've been diagnosed with a few mental illnesses, one being PPD or Paranoid Personality Disorder. When you think from a different perspective, it becomes easier to understand how someone so sweet and bubbly could be looked at as "crazy". No one wants to see the opposite side of the one that's always happy. PPD is an extreme personality disorder, in relation to one of the most commonly known extreme personality disorders, Obsessive Compulsive Disorder (OCD). Although I do not have OCD, PPD runs in the same family as far the "extreme" part goes. I either like you or I don't. You either love me or you hate me and for the most part, it's transparently on my face. Being a naturally paranoid person, I do not trust or let my guard down easily, despite the smile you may see. Trusting humans is single-handedly the most difficult thing for me to do because I am aware that people are naturally going to disappoint and betray. When around me in public, you'll notice that my head is always on a swivel. When around me in private, you'll notice how particular I am about certain things being a certain way.

- You're talking about illegal things? Lower your voice…
- You're smoking weed? Close the windows, blinds, and vents. (And we can't go out in public just yet…)
- You left cooking food unattended? What are you cooking?!
- Do you see this clean floor? Take your shoes off!
- You're looking this way pretty hard and long. That's a warning sign for danger… Say something or stop staring!
- You want ME to do it? Why?! When?! For how long?!
- Do I need any special skills or training?! Are you going to teach me?! Where are you going?!

I told you it all runs in the same family. On a positive note, I'm typically the first one to see danger coming and can reflect quickly in a fight or flight situation. Being paranoid and untrusting of my surroundings and the people in it may not be the most comfortable way to live, but I've learned to love and embrace the benefits for a healthy and happy lifestyle.

When it comes to the passion, it's fair to say that I'm a hard lover once my guard is actually down and one is considered to be trustworthy. I'm what many may know as a "ride or die" type of person. Extremely loyal and dedicated to the people who do right by me. This is my "crazy in love" because I don't have to be in love with someone to love them. My love is literally everything because I'm likely to do almost anything logical for someone I love. When my love is misused, abused or betrayed, the extreme opposite comes out of me and is mistaken for "crazy". I am the type of person who addresses issues through strong and direct verbal communication. One thing I know is if we can't respectfully talk about conflict and be willing to resolve it, you don't deserve my love at all. Many don't expect me to stand my ground on respect because they've only had the honor of seeing the bubbly side prior to testing my tolerance. You may put your foot down, but mine will always land in wet cement. Once you try me, you will never try me again because you'll be dismissed out of my life completely.

If nothing else is taken from this chapter, I believe the principle is to never underestimate anyone or their kindness. For someone like myself the love runs naturally for all living beings until you've given a reason to get cut off from receiving such a pure gift from God. I'd like to believe that learning and relearning yourself will always be an ongoing journey itself, especially if you're spiritual. Like many others, I still remain a humbled student of this journey called life. The scary key is not knowing or being aware of self-capabilities that can lead to death or imprisonment for anyone involved. This scary key is the sole reason I'm more at peace with dismissing someone out of my life. Today's society expects hurt and pain to be tolerated. Crazy, right? With instant gratification and social media playing a huge role in our current society, it's supremely easy to lose yourself. Or even worse, never learning your true self at all. I'd like to believe that everyone who is born is special in their own unique way. It was proven at the time of fertilization because you were the one of millions of sperm cells racing to do the exact same thing; Fertilize the egg for a chance at life. With that perspective, everyone is capable of something that no one else expects. Remember to be kind to this world and someday we may actually have a chance at World Peace. Certainly not in this generation, but the future can hold life changing greatness if you work hard enough. I'm living proof of that.

    My children, Cynveda and Cyrus, are also huge benefactors of my love and mental health growth. Without them, I would've had less to live for in the beginning, making death or imprisonment a higher likelihood. With them, I feel blessed. When you want the best for someone so badly that you make positive changes to your own behavior, that's love. As long as I'm breathing, I want to continue loving. Loving those who love me. Loving what I do. Loving myself.

ABOUT THE AUTHOR:

Social Media:

IG @empress.artic

Email empress@empressbianca.com

Empress Bianca, Single Mother, Multipotentialite, Philanthropist, Serial Entrepreneur, & Mental Health Activist, was born and raised in Cleveland, Ohio on September 7th in the early 90's. Some may know her as The Jacqueline of All Trades, while others know her as The Life of The Party, but many know her as both! She went from Administrative Assistant, to Executive Assistant, and then Licensed Insurance Producer. Empress excelled in both private and corporate environments, leading her to confidently chase entrepreneurial goals of her own. As a visionary, this experience fueled Empress Bianca to never stop striving for her passionate visions. As a young adult, Empress Bianca prioritized mental health awareness and she has holistically managed her mental illnesses. Empress Bianca became a brand for philanthropy and always bringing amazing energy to a party. In 2021, Empress Bianca started Anamnesis Entertainment & Beauty and Romance by Empress support, empower, educate and entertain others; especially minorities. She remains a student while sharing her knowledge and talents with quality individuals, businesses, networks, brands, and organizations by executing on planned community-based projects with a positive mission.

www.empressbianca.com

THE LOVE FOR OUR BLACK CHILDREN

Kennesha Wilson

As a black woman becoming an educator of young children is an especially important part of my life because I believe investing in our young people is the key to building strong black communities that children can grow in to become successful. What do I mean by investing in our children? Imagine what investing more in our children would do for the black community. I am not saying that we do not love our children and do not care about them, but we need to be supportive and knowledgeable, for all black children. If we become better advocators for children we will have stronger black communities for generations. Now we have opportunities to invest in our children because we are now investing more in ourselves. We are educating, making better health decisions, and working hard to provide better life opportunities for our families and communities. If we continue and support each other more, our children will make better decisions and do the same. Sometimes, we forget that children are the most important part of humanity.

You are probably thinking, how do we invest more into our children? We should start by respecting them. When I was a young person, I always thought "respect is not a given, it is earned."

I was wrong. As adults, we should always respect our children because they are modeling our behavior. When you give respect, it will be returned and appreciated. As a young parent, I did not understand this. I made some mistakes by not respecting my daughter's emotions and feelings. I thought that showing tough love would make her grow into a strong black woman, but respecting her feelings and emotions more would have made it easier for her to communicate with me when she became older. It probably would have made it easier for her to communicate better, in general. If we respect our children as important people, not just little objects we are responsible for, it will change our mindsets and the respect we have all together.

An essential way of investing and loving our black children is education. Educating ourselves and our children will help prevent us from being overlooked. We have become a driving force in our community and all the other communities as well. Yes, we have grown as a community over the years since the civil rights movement as important people by becoming educators, lawyers, doctors, politicians, scientists, artists, engineers, etc. What if we did more for education in our black communities?

I went to a party at my neighbor's house, a little over a month ago. She invited my family and a few other neighbors to celebrate her fiancé's birthday, or so I thought. We were having a good time drinking, listening to music, and talking. After being there for a while, her girlfriend shows up with her family (I probably would not have gone if I knew she was coming because she rubbed me the wrong way at the fourth of July cook-out we had). She is a black woman with two teenage children. I spoke about being a Pre-School teacher and how I enjoyed working with children. My neighbor's daughter was in the dining room area with her two children. We began to talk about our children. She states in the beginning of the conversation that she was going to get a shirt made with the words "Fuck them Kids" on it.

A few people laughed. I did not, because as an educator I did not find it funny. I looked around the room and into the dining room area where the children were. I could see that the comment made some of us feel uncomfortable. I continued the conversation by keeping it positive and stating how proud I was of my daughter for graduating high school and wanting to continue her education. I explained that I will be supportive of my daughter continuing her education and wanted to be able to help more with financing her education.

She stated that the only way her children would go to college is if they receive a scholarship. She would not sign any financial aid paperwork for them because she was not going to be responsible for the loan. I disagreed and informed her that she would not be responsible for the loans. She yelled in my face loudly that parents are responsible for the loans and if they needed someone to sign for them, they better ask their father. She went on to say that education is overrated.

I knew it was time to go because I did not want to ruin the neighbor's birthday. I responded that my daughter's father was deceased, and I would do whatever it takes for my daughter to become successful and happy. I was so pissed, I grabbed my stuff and left. The next morning, I was coming home from grocery shopping and my neighbor (who had the party) was leaving to go to the store. She apologized for her friend's behavior the previous evening. We talked about the kids and their feelings. We need that as black parents we needed to respect, love, and invest more into the children. This situation and conversation sparked something in me to think about loving and investing more into our black children.

In the black community, a lot of people feel that education is overrated and too expensive, but we need to change that mindset. If we change that mindset, we will be doing our children justice because education is the key to equality. I am not saying that going to college and incurring debt is the American dream, but as black parents we should save money for their education and future. If we stop buying things we do not need (partying, alcohol, expensive clothes/shoes etc.) we will change this stigma. If we saved only fifty dollars a paycheck, that would be more than twenty-one thousand dollars by the time they are eighteen. That could be enough to pay for trade school or one year of college. If we doubled or tripled that amount, imagine how that would encourage our children to further their education and help them start their lives without a lot of debt.

My daughter is eighteen now. She just graduated from high school and could have used some extra money for her college education. As a community, if we invest in our children's future, it would be beneficial for our young people. Encouraging and supporting our children to start a business or get the education they need, will open more doors in the black community. Education should never be considered overrated in the black community because so many people fought and died for this right.

I want to go back to educating our young children. Education starts from the time a child is born. Basic skills are learned from the people around us, not just in a classroom. Having positive role models is important for our young people. Education starts with language, physical, social-emotional, and cognitive (thinking and problem-solving skills) development. Positive role models such as parents (families), teachers, and people in the community who invest time in helping this development are contributing to young children's education.

My parents were not the best role models, but I had my grandparents. They did not go to college, but they were hard working, positive, loving people that took care of their family and helped people in the community. My grandparents went to segregated schools in the 1930s-40's. My grandfather graduated from high school, but my grandmother was the eldest of five siblings and sacrificed her education to care for her younger siblings. She had basic reading and writing skills and was able to help provide for her family. They might not have had a college education, but they were significant role models for me. They encouraged me to get my education and explained why it was important. They explained to me how education was a part of self-care and how important it was. I admire them for stepping up and being positive role models. I am so grateful for having them in my life. They helped raise me to become the strong black women I am today. Good role models are imperative to educating our black children.

Another way to invest and love our black children is providing better and positive life experience for them. When children have good life experiences, they tend to have better self-esteem and self-awareness. Providing better life experiences helps with development because children think in a more positive way. Life experience is not buying children items, but investing time to provide them with positive memories that will last a lifetime.

When I was working at a tech company, I met a well put together black woman. She shared with me that instead of buying her children gifts on Christmas, she took them on nice vacations. Each trip they took was designed to be a great life and learning experience for her children. They have traveled all around the world learning diverse cultures, eating different foods, and spending quality time with each other. I really admired that and thought it was a clever idea. We also talked about other life experiences she shared with her children that did not cost a lot of money like nature walks, art crafts with household items, and teaching them to cook. In our conversations she made me aware of how impactful positive life experiences are for our children. When they do not have them, it can be tragic. Think about it. If our children always have negative life experiences, what kind of perception of the world will they have? As a community we have the power to provide our children with better life experiences.

The key to investing in our black children is being more supportive of them. Our children need us to be present and involved in every process of their lives. Being supportive is essential to the growth and development of our children. When we support our children when they are young by recognizing and encouraging good behavior, it will lay the foundation for success. Our black children need and deserve the best support system we can offer them.

When I was young, my support system was not just my parents and grandparents. I had my big sister, educators, other family members, the church, and people in the community. When I was in high school, I had a tough time adjusting and transitioning due to issues in my household. My mother always stressed how important my education was. I could have used more support with decision making, life choices, positive life experiences, and having more positive role models in my life.

If it were not for my high school counselor, I would not have graduated high school. I was getting in trouble in school, skipping classes, fighting, and failing classes, but my counselor did not give up on me. She showed interest in me and genuinely wanted me to help me. I went to her office a lot because of my behavior. The first two years of high school I only received one and half credits total, you are supposed to have fourteen. During conversations with her I began to trust her. We discussed my family life and situation. We built a strong relationship because she showed interest in me. She pulled some strings for me and got me into the Thomas Edison Technology School. That is when things began to change in school for me. She even paid for my cosmology kit out of her own pocket.

I made the honor roll that year. She made sure I made up my credits by me attending night school, Saturday school, and summer school. She allowed me to do my community service hours in my high school main office. I did not graduate with my class, but I went back for half days the following year. I was a half of a credit short from graduating. I attended summer school and graduated with the night school and summer school students in a summer ceremony at another high school in the county. The ceremony was held on my nineteenth birthday. She was so proud of my dedication and hard work. She attended my graduation ceremony and brought me a gift. My mother, father, grandfather, little brother, and his girlfriend were there to support me. At that point, it was the best day of my life. My school counselor went above and beyond. I received my high school diploma because of her support and positive influence in my life. By being more involved and showing interest in the desires of our black children, we give them everything they need and more.

ABOUT THE AUTHOR:

Social Media:

IG @kekedmv1981

FB @kennesha.wilson

Email kennesha10@gmail.com

Accomplishments

- Founder and developer of K 4 Kare LLC. and Images by Kennesha
- Special certificates and awards in Early Childhood Education
- Child and Health Care Advocate
- Honor Roll Student

Kennesha Wilson was born and raised in Silver Spring, Maryland. She is a proud mother of one daughter. Kennesha has been a photographer for over twenty years. She has worked as a family portrait, school picture, and newborn baby photographer. Kennesha has a background in business and sales, maintaining a high-level service. She is currently working on her degree in Early Childhood Education. Kennesha owns a Home Care business and works in the education field as a Pre-school teacher. She enjoys working in the care business helping families meet their needs. She has a passion for working with young children and their families to provide the best care for them.

UNVEILING LOVE'S TRUE IDENTITY
MsVibrations

Love is a word that has many meanings yet so many people don't know what love means. I used to think love was something that could only be given by another person. Believing in fairytales, along with what society said, love was. Believing pain is love and going against what I wanted for myself was the sacrifice needed to bring me, love. If I were lucky enough, a man would love me too.

Love is supposed to be unconditional, uplifting, inviting, nonjudgmental, respectful, joyful, understanding, and always considerate especially when it involves other people. Accepting friendships and relationships that weren't aligned with what I wanted for my life showed me just how much love was lacking in every relationship, including the most important relationship, of them, all the relationship I had with myself.

We allow people to use and abuse us for the sake of love. We have a million excuses for why we stay in relationships with people that repeatedly hurt us. We say love is the reason that it's difficult for us to walk away and use that same word as a reason to stay.

If you ask me, no one truly knows what love is or what it means to completely love yourself. You won't know what love is until you have experienced everything love isn't or you are tired of getting the same results. That isn't love at all that's insanity. I had to learn that God is love and the way he loves me is how I needed to love myself.

God made me perfect in his image and said he would give me the desires of my heart. He is the creator of love and the Prince of peace. There's no way he would bring me pain. He wouldn't let me stay in any circumstance where love is not present. However, having free will isn't always free when you're the one paying the bill. We will make decisions based on contaminated love, then blame God for the choices we decided to make when he showed us in plain sight why something or someone wasn't good for us. God loves me unconditionally and always wants the best for me. I learned that loving myself before loving anyone else is a priority.

Before I can expect someone else to love me, I have to love myself and embrace all the things that I don't love about myself. I had to do the work and get to the root of the problem and pull them up one by one. Some of them even had thorns. I could change relationships but the one thing they have in common is me. What good is it to change the person if you aren't working on changing yourself?

Once I discovered where my pain lived that's when I began to nurture it with prayer, meditation, my life coach, God, and the key ingredient LOVE. I had to reprogram my belief system. I had to remember the truth and what God said love is.

I began to love myself and treat myself better, I started treating others better as well.

I learned to handle others with care and change the reflection of love within my heart. Out of your heart are the reflections of life and my heart was problematic. I was looking for answers from everywhere and spreading my issues from person to person; making them responsible for my pain. Without knowing it they became the keepers of my secrets.

I didn't understand how someone could love you and watch you cry, lie to you, disrespect you, call you out your name, then utter I love you and I believed it. The tongue speaks life or death. The person proclaiming to love me spoke such foul language. I had to take accountability for the part I played in every situation in my life. I had to forgive myself for everything I chose to tolerate and accept.

I had to be honest with myself and say, "Candice you don't love yourself because if you did there is no way you would accept anything less than what you deserve. If you truly loved yourself you would recognize that love and pain can't go together, especially when God is love and all good things come from the creator himself." I've learned, that I cannot control what others do. I can only control myself in every situation.

People meet us where we are. If they loved themselves they would be able to love me or recognize the love that poured from me onto them. Love is why I don't hold grudges and give people grace because that's the love God gives. When I started understanding love and being love I began attracting it in every area of my life. Love is the only universal law and I'm beyond grateful that I found it.

ABOUT THE AUTHOR:

Social Media:

IG @candicoatedsecrets

FB @candicoatedsecrets

Email candicoatedsecrets@gmail.com

www.candicoatedsecrete.com

Allow me to introduce myself, my name is Candice White, and I am a certified law of attraction coach. On July 18th, 2018, I decided to walk out on faith and started the "Candi Coated Secrets" Talk Show and Facebook group. I've been Featured in Voyage Baltimore Magazine, 92.Q, 93.9, 95.9, WRDB Media on IHeart Radio, and Canvas Rebel Magazine. I'm an affiliate for the luxury skincare line Renew You Body Butter and I have been on several billboards located in Georgia as well. I help people take the necessary steps to change their perception of life and create the life they want.

AS YOURSELF

NaTasha Tierra

Love, according to the New Oxford American Dictionary is:

1. an intense feeling of deep affection
2. a great interest or pleasure in something
3. A person that loves

While 1 Corinthians 13: 4-5 states that, "Love is patient, kind and without envy. It doesn't boast or dishonor others, it is not self-seeking. Love is not easily angered, it keeps no record of wrongs. It does not delight in evil but rejoices with truth. It protects, trusts, hopes and perseveres. Love never fails."

We have been taught by the world and the word what love is, but even "Uncle" Kirk recognized that "Few people really know what it means to really love somebody."

My understanding of love has evolved over the past ten years and if I am fortunate enough, God will continue to evolve my understanding of love even further.

Growing up in church I would always hear that we are called to love God with all our hearts and to love others. I did just that. I loved God by serving at church, going to Bible Study and applying what I learned to my life. I believed that if I did these things he would be pleased, know that I loved him completely, and trusted him with my life. Little did I know that all my God desired was time with me. He had created me perfectly for all he had called me to do. His only desire was for me to seek him first.

For others, I lived. If there was a need that I saw arise, I was the solution. If it wasn't within me I would seek to find it. The look on the faces of those who had received the relief was my reward. Seeing them find joy was my indicator that I was on the right page. I took this idea of Serving = Love into all of my relationships. Often giving beyond what I really should have, including my time, talents and resources.

Mark 12: 30-31 states that, "The greatest commandments are to love God with all your heart, soul and mind and to love your neighbors as yourself."

After many years of improper self-management, I realized that something was missing … the Love owed to me.

Prior to seeking and reading the word for myself, I tried to implement God's word from the understandings of others whose relationship with God I trusted, worship songs I heard and the messages that came from the pulpit. At times, some of those means led me down the wrong path of how to love and be loved.

There is a song, I won't say the artist, but the lyrics encourage us to Love God and Love people. Although this song was missing a very important part of the command (as yourself) it did highlight some suggestions that guided my actions around love. It expressed that you shouldn't have to strive for love and that love doesn't come from doing, it comes from being. This truth was a hard transition for me because I am a Doer. I provide solutions to problems. I have a passion to see people live their optimal lives. Inequity has fueled my passion for some time. I recognize that everyone does not have the same resources, but they must have access to them to have a fair chance.

You may have read what I just wrote and thought, what's wrong with that? Some may even have resonated with this or have commonalities within their own lives. Before you count your life as wrong, let me make clear that I do not see these attributes as wrong. I was just, out of order.

You see we are given the passion and purposes that we have for a reason. How we execute them determines our success. As the song goes, "I was loving God and loving people but not showing enough love to myself." If I can be honest … I wasn't really loving God.

Love God.

In order to love God we must know God. Love doesn't always feel like peaches and cream. The sweetness comes with victory, but in order to grow toward victory there must be a battle. God is our everything and as a result he loves us in the most holistic way possible. He shows us grace, mercy, love, trustworthiness, and faithfulness despite all we have done and will do. It's not about what we do but who we are. He is our creator, our Father, he delights in seeing us as we are. He enjoys our needs because it delights him to please us. It brings him joy when we come to him with our needs because we trust him. This love was commanded for us to know and receive first so that all else could flow from there. Attempting to love without first truly receiving love from God ensures that we will have limits in our love. I gave this unbiased, selfless love to people but ... I was out of order.

As Yourself

There is an old saying that "You can't pour from an empty glass and as my Mazda showed me, you can't drive a car with no oil!

The empty glass reference is cool. It shows us that if you aren't poured into you cannot give. But once the water is gone, the glass is still a glass. It can still be used. It just needs to be filled. In my life when I was like this, I would show up to serve the community, my family, and my relationships, but had nothing to give. Not taking the time to replenish myself had a direct correlation to how successful I was giving love. By showing up as the empty glass I was giving myself to my relationships physically, but they couldn't receive the benefits of who I was because I was empty.

No oil. Whew Chile. Here I was headed to celebrate the launch of Black Men Love. For several weeks, I had been notified by my car that it needed to be serviced. My to do list was driving my actions, and if I could start it, I would drive it. Well, that day I drove it and it broke down and locked up on me. It was no longer able to start and I couldn't get to my destination.

What's your oil? Has your body been trying to tell you that you are low on something? For me, my oil was rest! My body would give me indicators that it was time for rest, but if I could still get up and move her I did. You see, the needs were calling, and I had the solution! I was living for purpose and was ignorant enough to believe that if I died trying, it would be honorable, when it was foolish and not pleasing to God. I was so anxious for people to feel my love. I thought that sacrificing myself showed how deep my love ran. No! I found out that I was decreasing the number of lives I would impact and relationships I would have. I was shortening my life span due to lack of rest. I was also providing a horrible example for the people I was called to lead.

I was "driving my car without oil" in love. I was giving without ensuring that I was full first. In turn, my body broke down and locked up on me. I was struggling with high blood pressure, anxiety, depression, and PTSD. I prayed and asked God what I was doing wrong. He showed me his word. He told me that I was not just supposed to love others, but to love them As Myself. If I did not love myself there was a limit on what I would be able to give before I had nothing left. I strongly believe that most people were exposed to a negative view of self-care before a positive one. All the time, I hear that self-care was believed to be "selfish". God told me that it is not selfish but in fact a command. God knew that for us to fulfill the purpose he called and created us for we needed to remain full. He gave us rest to do just that, get a fill up!

The Shift

I had fallen in love. As a result, I had unconsciously become more and more of what my love wanted me to be, and less of myself. By the time I said I do, I was already sick and tired. Unbeknownst to many including myself, because of the seemingly invisible symptoms of depression and anxiety, I was suffering. I couldn't see myself beyond who I was for others, including him. As I found myself remembering who I really was and realigning, I became less of who he desired, and our process began. God brought me closer to him and his word during my separation. He showed me his commands. He made it clear to me why I was so depleted in my "well doing". I must love myself first! Taking care of me, knowing, loving, and respecting who I am are the things that will sustain me. I will then be able to do the same for others and receive the same from others. My giving nature that I was so proud of was attracting takers and pushing away the God ordained relationships that I needed. I was giving the love I was called to give out of order and receiving unfulfilling results.

Not anymore!

During the time of my separation, I gave myself to God. I emptied myself of all my beliefs and gave myself to him as a blank canvas. I prayed for him to show me the plans he had for me when he created me. I desired to seek his plan for my life and committed myself to walking his way. He took me on a journey of knowing him more, loving me more and not only to give but to be open to receive.

Now, I love God and allow myself to be loved by God completely. This process freed me from my belief that I had to do something to receive love. It was shattered as I began to see evidence in my life that God loved me just because I am me. He didn't love me any less if I made a mistake or did something wrong intentionally. (let's keep it real) Sometimes we choose to do wrong! Or maybe it was just me … But I digress. He loved me the same regardless of my actions. When I received this love, I began to love myself the same.

Shame and guilt fell off. The enemy couldn't use that to distract me from purpose. To keep me in a pit of self-pity. I loved myself! I began to love my wrong turns as God showed me even those would be used for his glory. (Romans 8:28)

This love transferred over to others. I love others freely without bias or judgement. I love others for who they are, not what they do. I understand that if allowed, God will move in all their circumstances, even the ones they walked into themselves.

My love is patient and kind. It seeks no wrongs but seeks to work through it all with God at the center. My love is open to receive with gladness. My love desires to be submissive to my love that loves and is led by God. I don't love with restraints and fear but with freedom and expectancy.

I love more freely knowing that hurt is not something that can be avoided but when God is in it, it becomes a refining fire instead of one sent to burn! I love more freely because I opened myself up to love. I sat before God and sought his deepest intentions for me and love. I wrote it down and made it plain as he instructed me during my intimate time with him as well as in his word from Habakkuk 2:2. When love walked into my life, I was able to see it and receive it.

I know a love that loves me for who I am and who I am to be, not all that I do.

This is the Love I desire for You. The love from God, the love from others and of course... the Love from You!

ABOUT THE AUTHOR:

Social Media:

IG @iamnatashatierra

FB @natasha.tierra

Email Ntbrown1017@gmail.com

NaTasha Tierra is a Woman of God, called and chosen to fulfill her purpose to free others as she has been freed. She believes that this is a call for us all, to take the lessons in which we have learned, reach out to another and teach them.

NaTasha is a Serial Social Entrepreneur, Speaker, and Author who uses her gifts, skills, and talents to better her community and those in it. She is a servant first. She activates the communities of Baltimore and those who love them to do the same by sharing and participating in community building events and activities.

Her passion is to see everyone have an equitable opportunity to live the lives of purpose they were created to live. Her organization B. HER Solution serves as an intermediary for our service providers and the communities in which they serve. With such a rich network of creative learning experiences and resources they will be the number one network for quality service for young girls and their families. In addition, B. HER Solution provides coaching to social entrepreneurs' that desire to make an impact in the lives of young girls. We believe that to serve a girl, is to serve a nation for that, is what she will give birth to.

A former Baltimore City Juvenile Case Manager, former Baltimore City Public School (BCPSS) Teacher with a Bachelor of

Arts in Sociology from The Hampton University, NaTasha Tierra is a Catalyst for Change.

MY FIRST LOVE

Robyn Christian

Growing up I was a Daddy's girl! I would hang out with my Dad and his friends. He would talk to me about boys and life. I am the middle child of five, and the oldest of the second set of kids. My Dad made sure I wanted for nothing! He always said, "Babygirl, if a man can't do for you what I can or more, then he's not worth your time. You were raised with standards and your Mom gave you a church background, don't settle for a bum man."

As I grew into womanhood, I always kept his words in mind. Looking back, his words were just that in my mind! I tried to pick good guys, family-oriented, trying to reach their dreams like me. Instead, I chose guys that initially appeared to be what I wanted, but they were "street boys" trying to be what I wanted. I remember speaking with my Dad and asking him why do I choose these guys? He said with so much remorse, "Maybe we held you too tight! Maybe I put too much pressure on you to date a certain type of guy."

I told him, "Don't worry Dad. I'm tough enough to handle this! These are all lessons for when I meet the guy for me."

Fathers are important. Fathers set the tone for what women tolerate, the love women will accept, and the forgiveness women can give a man when he falls short. I love my Dad, but as a husband, he was a cheater and a womanizer. Those are traits that I do not accept! There was a point in my life that I believed that if I loved my man and was present in the relationship, he should deal with my cheating. For many years, I kept two men in my life at the same time. For me, men were not capable of being the whole package. A man may be good in bed, but not capable of providing or being present in a relationship.

As I've gotten older and participated in therapy, I realized my problem. I fell in love with the image of my Dad. I downplayed all of his underlying issues (drug addict, womanizer, paranoid schizophrenic) and was willing to accept them because he was loving, present and a provider. I had to come to grips with the fact that my Dad was supposed to be all of those things to me. I was expecting guys that didn't have a role model in their lives, who never took care of anything in their lives, and believed that women are only good for sex, to handle me with care. They couldn't. After years of celibacy and therapy, I am finally in a place where I can have a balanced and monogamous relationship.

ABOUT THE AUTHOR:

Social Media:

IG @robynachristian

FB @robyn.christian.38

Email robyn_christian38@yahoo.com

Robyn Anetrice Christian. The fifty-year-year-old mother of two adult children, divorced, retired Law Enforcement Officer Corporal has been a community business owner for over ten years. Ms. Christian has had an extensive background in providing services to the Community, from working for Baltimore City Child Support Enforcement to Virginia Beach Law Enforcement. In 2016, Ms. Christian started a Mother & Baby holistic housing program called Anetrice House, Inc. In 2021 she started a program for the youth called Mending Broken Wings, LLC. In 2004 Ms. Christian became an Investigator for the Department of Public Safety and Correctional Services. She retired in 2022. Ms. Christian is the 2024 Democratic Candidate for Baltimore City's City Council 2024

OH, TO BE BOUNDLESS

Samantha Hutchison

They tried to ride on my wings,
But there was nowhere to go.
You can borrow my strength,
But you can't use my soul, no you can't use my soul.

I am thinking of a time when there was no sorrow,
Only the silk laughter of little brown girls playing in the summer.
Colorful beads, matching dresses, bouncy coils, skin glistening...
Pay attention, make sure you are listening
Because I am telling you the story before innocence was captured,
Before courage was suffocated, and
Before time was hijacked.
Before hope was dehydrated and safety was ruined.

I am remembering the time before heartache sunk into marrow, and love spoiled in the sun.
When life was more than a box of chocolates, and sweeter than the bitterest piece.

I am telling the story of a thousand years.
A thousand symphonies rising in the key of "I ain't got time"
To mince words,
To lower expectations,
To think fearfully,
To move slowly,
To speak quietly.

I am telling you the story of la chica negra
Su amor, su dolor, y su libertad.

That is to say,
Her love, her pain, and her freedom.

To be a black woman and love boundlessly is to be courageous,
Knowing that the world will not understand you though they be touched by the life in your hands.

It is a conundrum,
Yet a constant reward.

It is living in the paradox of knowing your passion will always be mistaken as rage.

Your pain as sensitivity,
And your voice as meaningless banter,
But who cares anyway?

Sisters, tell me
Have you ever wanted to just scream out at the top of your lungs just to see if someone is listening?

Unleash the anger of your oppression to the wind,
Praying she will carry it to your oppressor
And make them taste the blood of their own violence.

Yeah, I do.
I believe that inside of the screams of little black girls, their fighting hands, and their running feet,
Is a deep, deep yearning to be seen, to be heard, and to be understood.

What does innocence mean when everyone around you is sowing lies,
Telling you that the dreams will never rise,
That your sons will never shine,
And your daughters have no need for tears.

Their childhoods are sent into an abyss of metal prisons and Ivory cages.

Time and time again we dig them out with our broken arms and bruised hands.

All the while we wonder,
Why our innocence has to fade?
Why do we have to keep our mouth silent?

And love secretly, mourn secretly, yet hate openly.

Why?

Why do we keep getting winter when we told you we wanted Spring!

When does suffering come to an end after death, after sickness, after insanity?
When does it come to an end?
Where does the home of strong live?
Where does Strong go to lay her head, to find rest and to find hope?

How does she access the sun when the moon keeps hogging her sky?
If she had a song I bet you it would sound something like this...

Singing...

I'd like to know what it feels like to stand on the sun, and wrap my arms in the daylight, to see where love comes from.

I'd like to know what it tastes like to breathe in the Light,
And sing the song of the morning, to know what hope feels like.

I have always wondered about love.
What it is and what it isn't.
How it plays hide and seek with my blackness,
And touch and go with my soul.

Skips time on the rhythm of my heart,
And beats against the shores of my sisters hope.

To be a black woman and love boundlessly,
Is to render yourself to vulnerability,
While keeping the bone firmly standing in your back
So that your purity won't be tainted, pulled, and destroyed.
So that your strength won't be stolen, and your glory won't be put out on display.

To be a black woman and love boundlessly is to grant yourself permission to breathe.
Walk it slow, and keep it still.
Knowing that your breath is a sign of freedom.

Woman, there is solitude within your ability to let go.

You can't carry the weight alone,
You can't fix it all.

But you can just be.
You can just be you.
You can do just what you can.
You can just lend without breaking yourself in half.

You can just say no.
You can just say yes.
You can just say maybe idk I'll get back to you.

You can be loud.
You can be silent.

Baby, you can be you and let the chips fall where they land.

Oh, to be a black woman and love boundlessly.

Lately, I've been very tender, a well of tears shut up in my heart.
Now washing and washing the guilt away.

Rushing out of their captivity and forcing me to be opened.

I sat for a moment,

Then,

God breathed and a mountain of stone came falling down,
I saw my heart turn to water and the ground before me to embers.
Unwrapping the chords from my mind,
Removing the shackles from my predisposition.

And I finally opened my mouth,
Stared my giants right in the eyes and said, "let go of me."

I will not let them charge me for something I did not buy, break, or bend.
My blackness is too precious to be sold.
I am writing this keeping all the black women I know in mind.
The ones who made magic out of misery,
The ones whose hands made dinner,
Whose accounts bought shoes, clothes, and food.
The ones who did the best they could with what they were given.
The ones who wanted to rest in green pastures, but were met with stone walls along the way.

I am thinking of my sisters, who dared to dream but were told to shut up and starved themselves out of joy.

I am thinking about my mother who kept all the dreams and desires she had locked in her heart, away in a little box,
So that they wouldn't be stolen.

I'm thinking of my friends and their mothers, always working hard
even when hard-working was nothing and never enough.

To be a black woman and love boundlessly is to be a witness,
See the pain of your community and love it back to life.

See the darkness in your sister's eyes and offer them light.

To be a black woman and love boundlessly is to turn your back on shame,
Embracing the beauty that comes with the truth.

And the truth is that no one,
No one else
Was made like you.
They tried to ride on our wings,
But there was nowhere to go.

We tell them,
You can borrow our strength,
But you can't use our soul
No you can't use our souls.

Oh, to be a black woman and love boundlessly,
Is to be free.

This poem is dedicated to all the young black girls who, for all it's worth, deserve to give and receive love boundlessly. This poem is dedicated to black women across the world who yearn for their stories to be seen, heard, and acknowledged, who are weary and just want rest. This is for the inner child, inside of me and inside of you, that has been locked away for years. She needs to know that there is still time for her to love and be loved boundlessly. To all my beautiful black queens, don't be afraid to love and receive fearlessly and passionately, you are worth that and more.

Samantha Hutchison

ABOUT THE AUTHOR:

Social Media:

IG @Gettingwellwithsam

FB @samantha.hutchison.5

Email shutchisonbooking@gmail.com

Samantha Hutchison is a singer, songwriter and poet born and raised in Southern California who has now been living in the DMV for over eleven years. Samantha became interested in music at an early age. She began writing music and poetry at the age of twelve as a means of therapeutic expression. Samantha's creativity has been inspired by her faith in Christ and a myriad of challenging life experiences and social injustices as well as her fiery passion for beauty and art. Samantha is an advocate for social change and a licensed mental health clinician in the state of Maryland. Her mission is to spread the message of love, hope, and healing creatively through the gospel of Jesus Christ and the ministry of mercy.

THAT "AS IS" LOVE

Shaniece Watkins

Love - an intense feeling of deep affection. A great interest and pleasure in something. Feel deep affection for (someone). Like or enjoy very much.

In my freshman year of high school, I was outed by someone my Mom knew. My Mom was and is a bring it to the source kind of person, so she did just that. She asked me. As a young, scared, ignorant high school student, I denied it. Deep down she knew, because she told me not to lie, so I cried and told her the truth. She had questions. She was concerned, confused, and hurting. This was new for both of us.

"Did someone touch you inappropriately?"

"No."

"Was it something I did?"

"No."

"Where did this come from?"

"I don't know."

I wanted this conversation to end. Seeing the tears roll down my Mom's face destroyed me. How could I do this to her? Why am I not like everyone else? Is something wrong with me? Why do these feelings even exist in me? I wasn't raised this way. I did not grow up seeing these things. Maybe I can pretend and suppress my feelings, but the thought of that made me feel sick.

Our encounters after that discussion surprised me. She didn't treat me differently. She didn't look at me differently. I was still allowed to be around my siblings. She still loved me and talked to me. It was almost as if nothing changed. I could still see the worry on her face at times. It's almost like she was somewhere lost in the unknown, the how come, the what happened. She needed time! As did I. This was a process. A new introduction to life for the both of us.

Over time we had conversations. In those conversations I was always reminded that I was loved no matter what. To never ever feel like I must hide myself or anything that I'm going through from her because I'm her child. That nothing in life will ever stop her from loving me. She told me that she doesn't have to agree with everything that I do, but she will always be present! She made me promise her that I would come to her if I was ever in need and I did! I had a safe space where I could be me without judgement. Without fear. I wasn't alone. I was loved in the purest way that you could ever be loved. As is.

Of course, I started dating and my Mom loved on my first girlfriend like she birthed her. Sleepovers were out of the question, but my relationship was allowed to be a normal high school love affair. We were given guidance when we were struggling, a stern talking to when we were misbehaving, and extra love when we needed it. We were allowed to grow.

Now I'm married. I have a son that was conceived through IUI and the family I created gets to share that love. Fortunately, I married into a family that loved on me just as my Mom did. Through this I learned that I am privileged. My wife, my son, and I are privileged. We have what most people are lacking, love.

In the LGBTQ+ community many children are refused and isolated from the families they were born into. They are forced to figure things out on their own without the village that it takes to raise a child. They are mishandled and left without guidance during a time in life where the struggle is certainly real. Many may not believe this, but the internal battle that you endure from just having these attractions are hard. You are already your own critic. You have questions, you feel guilty, you don't understand, you are still trying to figure this out. It's literally an internal battle. Adding that to being banished from the very people who are supposed to love you is its own beast. Am I not good enough? Do I not deserve love? Will my family ever love me again? Should I just not be me in order to gain their love?

This wasn't my story, but hearing these stories compelled me to reach out to my Mom via text. I asked her if she would be okay being the "Gay Mom." Because I'm hardly ever serious she thought I was playing. I quickly called her and explained what I saw, what I've heard, how these stories made me feel, and how vital our relationship has been in so many ways. I thanked her for being her. For loving me no matter what. For not giving up on me, even though I know this was a struggle. For allowing me to grow and being there to guide me along the way. Because of her, I'm not lacking love, so I'm not searching for it and tolerating the residuals of it. I know so many who are though. They need her and if she is willing, I would like to share her so others can experience love. She agreed with no hesitation and has since "adopted" her first 3 LGBTQ+ children. I have a cousin who also joined us on this journey. We saw a need for a village and decided to open our doors! What is life without love?

I say all that to say that love isn't pain, rejection, judgment, or having all the answers. It isn't always easy. Love is patience, humility, empathy, morality. It is always deeper than surface level and having it in your life is vital. It is an action, the key ingredient, the razzle dazzle, the sauce. When you have it you will know, and when you lack it, it'll show.

Four letters, so much meaning, so much character (distinctive to an individual), so much expectation, the known, the unknown, the physical, the mental, the emotional, the individually defined.

This is my first most impactful experience with love and if you are reading this and this is remotely close to your story we are here. You are not alone. We will love on you properly. We will value you and you are invited to our village.

Interview with Mom (Mom's Viewpoint)

How did you find out?

When I went to your high school for a conference after you were suspended. I was really lost in the sauce when the principal was explaining the situation. He started explaining a story about kids committing suicide for not being accepted. I was just sitting there trying to figure out what that had to do with you. I think he was really trying to tell me that you were gay because the whole altercation happened between a bunch of gay girls that you were hanging out with. I remember asking you about it and you didn't say anything. Your eyes started tearing up and I knew it was true.

What was your initial reaction when you found out? How did you feel?

Confused. This was my biggest feeling. A little hurt because I didn't imagine I would have a kid in the LGBTQ+ community. So many kids were doing it at the time that I thought it was just a phase. Like something you were experimenting with.

How would you describe the process from the beginning until now? Was there a time frame for you to think/process it? Did you have someone to confide in in during this process?

There was no specific time frame. I took a while to process it. It was not easy to process that information. It took me a couple of years to get past the feeling of it. Maybe around two years. It was a process to get from one thing to the next. I had my best friends Bunny and Juneen to talk to. I reached out to them.

What was it like having to express this to family/friends?
Embarrassing at the beginning. I felt embarrassed by it. Then I didn't know how to explain it. Sometimes people have questions you cannot answer. I only felt that for a small time because I wasn't sure if you were really like that. I thought it was just a phase. I didn't want to get comfortable with it then you be unsure. Until I was sure that you were sure, I wasn't taking it seriously.

Do you or have you ever felt like something happened in my life that led to me being a lesbian?
Yes. I was unsure if someone had touched you in the beginning. I thought that me being in a bad relationship and you watching me go through a lot of stuff maybe turned you off from men.

Is there anything that you would do different?
Be more open to conversation and listen in the beginning. At the beginning I wasn't listening. I was just speaking. I would have stopped trying to think about what I think your life should be and accept what you chose while giving you space to figure it out.

Has your perception of the LGBTQ+ community changed since I came out?

Yes, it has. It gave me a better understanding. A lot of times you take guesses about the way things are in the LGBTQ+ community. Having you opened me up to more information.

What are some challenges you have faced during this experience? How did you overcome said challenges?

Coming across people who are homophobic. I feel like this is one of the biggest challenges I have and accepting that this is your lifestyle. When I come across homophobic people, I do my best to explain to them. It doesn't always work, but who gives a shit because they don't have to live your life.

How do you respond to prejudice? What is it like for you when you hear or see me experience prejudice? How do you comfort me after the fact?

Well, when I hear prejudice, I try to correctly inform. If they don't budge, I leave them to their own vices. You are so comfortable in your own space that you don't need to be powder puffed. You are comfortable in your own skin so it doesn't matter what the outside thinks. As long as you know you are loved by those who matter we won't let outside forces infiltrate us.

Do you have worries in reference to your grandson being raised in a same sex household? Do you have any worries when it comes to me being a lesbian?

No, because he's loved thoroughly. No. The only worry I have is outside people who might react off their beliefs. I don't really worry about you because I know that you will take care of yourself.

Did you educate yourself about the LGBTQ+ lifestyle? If so, how?

By sitting down with you and asking some of your counterparts questions. You see who I call when I have questions.

What have you learned from this experience?

Love is love. Love doesn't come with rules. Love doesn't pick and choose. Love doesn't care if you are a man or a woman. Love is love period. People put stipulations on it.

What was your initial reaction to me asking you to be the "gay mom?" What made you say yes?

It was funny to me because I'm up here thinking I'm not gay, but I am a mom, so I was like what does that mean. I'm excited about it. The whole thought of it is exciting, because to be able to open up your heart and share the love and support that someone else may need is everything. It's bigger than you and me. I thought it was a great idea. Being able to give someone love could make the biggest difference in their life. I think it's even better that we get to do this together.

What advice do you have for parents who may be struggling to accept their child being LGBTQ+?

Put love at the beginning of everything. Do more listening to understand versus listening to respond. Always know that it is not your life to live. It is theirs. You love them through it because you birthed them. They're yours.

ABOUT THE AUTHOR:

Social Media:

IG @shaniece_watkins

Email shaniece.t.watkins@gmail.com

Shaniece Watkins grew up in Baltimore, Maryland. She is a medically retired Army Veteran. She is a proud employee of her four-year-old son's business, C.H.A.Y.N.G.E. LLC. She is currently looking to go back to school to pursue her doctorate degree in Sexology. She is a devoted wife of ten years and the mother of an amazing four-year-old boy. Shaniece believes that you should show up as you are and not the representative that you created in your times of survival! You will never fully experience the future if you don't heal from the past while making time for the present. Our strength shouldn't be defined by how much we can endure. Don't become the shook-up soda bottle because you chose to mask pain as strength. Also, the get it out the mud mentality should be perceived as poison to the minds of black people. There's no glory in generations and generations of people starting from scratch. Let's change the trajectory of that!

THE LOVE EXPERIENCE

Toyre Davis

Self-Sacrifice

Who can wipe a tear that will not fall? Emotions; suppressed them all.
Sometimes when we think of love and we think of being wanted, being cared for, or even being accepted. Make no mistake, this is not just relating to a significant other. These feelings often relate to friends, family, work or even community. It's a hard thing loving something or somebody that doesn't love you back.

Love unrequited selfless in its giving. Black Women Love.
Always Available. Always Accommodating. Always Giving. Black Women Love.
Pouring from an empty cup expecting it to be full. Black Women Love.

Accepting the unacceptable, even when it hurts. Black Women Love.

Standing in the gap for those who are no longer around. Black Women Love.

Silent cries for help that often go unheard. Black Women Love.

Showing up for everybody except for yourself. Black Women Love.

Enough is enough. Black Women Love.

The battle is not yours. Black Women Love.

Self-Aware

The past never sees the future and anything you compromised to gain you will eventually lose. At this point, it's about being the best version of you for you and recognizing your true value. Discounting is not an option as a price has already been paid. It costs what it costs. How much have you already spent and how much more are you willing to pay? See the process is the cost of admission but most won't spend the time. Focus on you and it will be worth every dime.

Forgive yourself. Black Women Love.

Give up who you were to find out who you are. Black Women Love.

Take a step back and get the big picture. Black Women Love.

Let go of guilt for the goals you didn't reach. Black Women Love.

Decide to be free. No going back. Black Women Love.

Stop worrying about what people think. Black Women Love.

Find your voice and never back down. Black Women Love.

Feel free to standout. Black Women Love.

Plan your work and work your plan. Black Women Love.

Get rid of every unnecessary thing. Black Women Love.

Stand firm and grounded. Black Women Love.

What you see on the outside is a reflection of what's going-on on the inside. Black Women Love.

You will always act like the person you think you are. Black Women Love.

Get out of your comfort zone. Black Women Love.

This too shall pass. Black Women Love.

Self-Love

You'll only reap to the level you feel worthy. You definitely want to keep this in mind. If you let someone else assign your value, you'll lose every single time. Honoring yourself is when everything will change. Let go of the fear of rejection and watch your world rearrange. Give yourself permission to flow divinely in who you are. Don't mute yourself for anybody you've come too far.

Take care of you. Black Women Love.

Keep pressing until you produce. Black Women Love.

Keep moving forward. Black Women Love.

No stagnation. Black Women Love.

Live on purpose. Black Women Love.

Act on what you believe. Black Women Love.

Align your strategy with your plan. Black Women Love.

Be mindful of the things you take in. Black Women Love.

Inwardly adorn. Black Women Love.

Let your wisdom decide your relationships. Black Women Love.

Never allow the sun to go down on your anger. Black Women Love.

Be a student of your environment. Black Women Love.

Not everybody can go with you. Black Women Love.

To whom much is given, much is required. Black Women Love.

And it came to pass… Black Women Love.

Black Women Love

As black women our love cannot be summed up as a feeling, in what we do or even what we experience. Love is much more than that. Love is the driving force of who we are. You see we must love ourselves before we can love anyone else. Just like on a plane you're instructed to put on your mask first or risk dying trying to save someone else. It's the same concept. I submit to you, love is not only how we relate to others, but more importantly how we relate to ourselves. Keep your love tank full, because self-love is going to save you every time.

-BWL

ABOUT THE AUTHOR:

Social Media:

IG @WhoIsToyre

Email toyrespeakslife@gmail.com

Who is Toyre? A community advocate who is passionate about the well-being and development of people and community. She actively gives back by educating underserved communities about financial literacy and connecting people to resources. As a mentor, she is the voice of reason to many. She has been featured on several podcasts. She is a serial entrepreneur who works in the financial services industry and is also a small business owner. A lover of nature and an enthusiast of the arts… music, theater, visual, you name it. It is her delight to find joy in the little things and inspiration in everything. Her motto is, "do unto others as you would have them do unto you." How she presents is exactly who she is.

I HATE THAT I LOVE YOU

Yendi A Jones

I'm beautiful. I'm powerful. I'm strong. These are my daily affirmations that roll across my screen every morning when I wake up. It's funny, I used to think affirmations were a waste of time. As if looking in the mirror every morning and saying positive words about yourself are supposed to make you believe that you like what you see. I hear people talk about how they wake up every morning, say their affirmations, meditate, and repeat daily, and it sets the tone for the rest of their day. It took me dealing with my own issues and learning about myself. Now I appreciate daily meditation and affirmations that taught me to love me and the skin that I am in.

Growing up in the 90's, being plus size was nothing to be proud of. Let's face it, on TV it was taboo. You already knew that if you were going to sit on the front row at a comedy show that you better have thick skin, because the first person they were coming for is the fat one. Growing up, I was the only one in my group who was "healthy", that's what I always like to refer to as being plus size. I didn't really have any plus size friends until I got into high school. I developed early, I was in a bra at seven and developed hips at the age eleven. I was the thickest one out of all of my friends. My friends used to call me bear paws because I was heavy handed and there were a few times where people would tease me because of my size.

I could never wear what everyone else was wearing. Torrid and Fashinova were not around yet, so I had to make do with what I had. My mom would take me places like Sears. My dad's friend used to own a clothing store that would sell a lot of no name designers and I would wear men's shirts and jeans to school to cover up. It's hard to have confidence and build yourself up when someone is always trying to knock you down and make you feel some type of way about yourself. Looking back at my pictures from when I was younger, I wasn't even that big, but a girl my size was out of the norm.

The worst day was when I was in middle school in gym class, and they had to weigh us in front of everyone. My first thought was, "What idiot thought this was a good idea?" My second thought was, "How can I get out of this horrifying event." Unfortunately, it had to be done and I was not able to get out of it. After that day it was all downhill. Kids would start to tease me in the hallway when I walked by. I will never forget how this one kid would always yell earthquake and then would fall to the ground. Of course, I punched him in the face. I may have gotten teased, but I always knew how to fight back. On the outside I tried to not let it get to me, but I would still go home every day and cry to my parents about how the kids at school would make me feel.

In the early 2000's my relationship with my body went left. I have always had a love-hate relationship with my body. The majority of the time there was more hate than anything else, but for some reason the relationship was getting worse. The little girl who was once obsessed with staring at herself in the mirror began looking at herself as if her body was the enemy. I began to start tearing myself down. When I looked at myself in the mirror, I would always find something that I didn't like, everything from the flap of my arms to the ripples on my thighs. God why do I have to have such wide hips or sheesh I wonder how I can get rid of these fat rolls in the back. I would be out with my sisters or my mom, and see someone else plus size, and ask if that's how I looked? It was terrible. I was miserable. I was my worst critic.

My mom has always told me since I was a little girl, "You cannot help that God was kind to you."

As if that was supposed to make me feel any better. I hated the summer because I knew that I would never go out in shorts and tanks I would always wear long sleeve shirts and jackets with pants.

My friends would always ask me the same stupid question, "Oh my gosh aren't you hot?" or "Why do you always wear those winter clothes?"

I would always reply with, "Oh, I am actually not that hot." Meanwhile, inside I was dying of heat stroke. I wish I would have listened to my mom more when I was younger about not being concerned about what other people think about me and wearing whatever I wanted to wear. I have learned as an adult that people really do not care about what you're doing or what you have on. If they do, then you must be doing something right.

Growing up I was into cheerleading. It was my life. I started at five and cheered all the way through middle school. My freshman year, I decided to take a little break and try to explore other options, but I could not stay away. My sophomore year I decided to try out for Junior Varsity, I knew I was going to make it. My cartwheel game was not strong, but you could not tell me anything when it came down to busting out those splits. After tryouts I found out that I made the team but there was just one problem. The uniform was not made for someone with curves. My high school did not want to order a uniform in my size. My mom was forced to find a seamstress who was able to make some adjustments so that I could fit into my uniform. At first, I was a little upset. Could you blame me? It felt like I was the only plus size girl who had ever been on the squad. I decided to embrace it. Honestly, I thought I looked cute in my uniform. I felt like at this moment my body and I were in a good place in our relationship.

That all changed my Junior year and Varsity raised enough money to buy new uniforms. I thought that maybe this was my chance. When I made it to Varsity, I could finally get a uniform ordered that would fit me. That was a joke. The uniforms that were ordered were all they had. They did not have enough to order new ones. I did not make the Varsity team. I was devastated because I worked so hard. A part of me felt like the reason that I did not make it was because they did not have the budget to order a uniform to fit my size. I wish I had the fight in me back then because I would have raised hell. My mom did go to the superintendent and the head of the athletic department, but I did not want her to make a big deal out of it. I just wanted to be done with that school, so what did she do? At the end of my junior year when the cheer season was over, she took my uniform apart and gave it back to them in pieces. That was her way of sticking it to the man. I appreciate her for that.

As I got older it seemed like nothing had changed between us, in fact my relationship with my body got worse. It was borderline toxic. I tried to fix my body. I went on a diet and failed. I tried working out and failed. I even tried not eating and failed. I just got heavier. I felt like no matter what I did I just couldn't change how I felt about myself. Until one day I decided to throw in the towel and accept defeat. I stopped taking full body pics of myself. I started to only wear leggings and size 4XL men's sweatpants. They were my comfort clothes. If you went through my wardrobe, you would see that everything I owned was in black. I was in a good place. No self-hate. Just a nice healthy relationship between me and my body. It lasted for five years. I didn't have a scale, so I had no clue how much I weighed. I even went out and got my bellybutton pierced and felt so confident.

We were happy. Until I found a new primary care doctor and had to stand on the scale. When I stepped on the scale it was time for me to face reality. It seemed like my weight was too far gone and all those bad feelings came rushing back. I was fat. A round ball that waddled everywhere I went. I was miserable again. This time I felt like there was no way that I could shake this feeling. That was until I met my therapist and joined a Facebook group that was all about helping black women love themselves. This group was everything. I met so many women who were just like me. Some were going through bad breakups and lost all the love they had for themselves. Some were like me. Lacked confidence, body shamed themselves, and felt lost. This group talked about everything from mental health issues, setting up small meetups, and even introduced me to meditation. I noticed that most of the girls in the group would talk about how great their therapist was at helping them overcome the issues they were having. Now in our community, mental health issues are something that we never want to talk about. A lot of times, we will just say, "Give it to God and pray on it."

I did not think going to a therapist would help me, but I'm glad that I listened to my inner self and searched for a therapist near me. There were not a lot of black therapists in my area, but I stumbled across my therapist's profile. She helped with building confidence, she practiced yoga, and she was a Zumba instructor. I decided to give her a try and see what she was all about. I must admit that at first it was a little awkward. I had no clue what to talk about with her. To be honest I thought I was wasting my time. I was wrong, seeing my therapist every two weeks taught me so much about myself and the issues I have.

I learned how important it was to celebrate small victories. For example, I decided to give working out another try. Even though I could only work out for five minutes, I still celebrated the fact that I gave it a try. My therapist showed me how to look in the mirror and instead of finding something negative to say about myself, look at myself and find something positive. I now look at myself and say things like, "Girl I see you have nice skin." or "I really did my thing today when I picked out this outfit."

I decided that instead of trying to lose weight because I'm not happy with myself and forcing all these goals. I now work out and eat right because it makes me feel good. Who cares what the scale says. It doesn't mean that you're not doing your thing and don't let it make you feel defeated. I started journaling and writing down how I feel about myself. I started changing the negative words into something uplifting. Every day I set a timer to spend at least two hours listening to meditation music and journaling. It's nice to unplug for a bit and focus on myself. Since social media has become so popular, we spend so much time seeing what other people have or how they look. We become obsessed, thinking that's how we should be living our lives or that's how we should look. I have noticed that since I have stopped spending time on particular social media platforms, I've stopped body shaming myself.

There is something that I always hear from my friend's wife telling their kids every Sunday. She says that it's a day to reset and get ready for the week. I decided to take what she said and apply that to myself. I am thirty-eight years old, and I want to use these last two years in my thirties to reset and get myself prepared to turn forty. All the insecurities, the anxiety, and low self-esteem. I do not want to carry that into my forties. I wanted to change the person that I was, reset and start over. To help me achieve that, I started doing yoga to help me build my confidence and boost self-awareness. Since starting yoga, I have learned to accept myself and stopped comparing myself to other people. Yoga has taught me a lot about my body, has helped me feel empowered, and relieves stress. I am not afraid to push myself to the limit with yoga. When I fall, and believe me, I fall quite often doing different positions, I learn to get back up and keep trying. I am a huge advocate for yoga. I started to take the time to educate myself and learn more about it, including the different styles and health benefits. I feel the same with meditation. It has helped me a lot with my anxiety. Every evening before bed I take the time to meditate and relax. I find that nightly meditation helps me sleep better and I wake up with a lot more energy. Rupaul has a saying at the end of every episode of Drag Race, and that is, "If you can't love yourself, how in the hell you gonna love somebody else?"

That statement sticks with me every day. I learned on this journey that if you're not in love with yourself then it is going to be hard to love someone else. The one thing that I did not want to do is go into a new relationship with someone feeling the way that I feel about myself and bringing in all of these insecurities. I have learned in therapy that it is not your partner's responsibility to make you feel confident and secure, and it is also not their job to make you feel happy when you are not happy with yourself. You do not need anyone to constantly tell you how beautiful you are to make you feel good about yourself. If you know you are beautiful and you believe it then it is not a requirement for someone to remind you every day. So much about me has changed over the past few years. I stopped caring about what other people have to say about me, what I wear and how I look has nothing to do with you and you do not even pay my bills so why do I care. Last year I went to Mexico and wore a bathing suit on the beach without a shirt. This past summer I wore shirts and even short skirts and started showing my legs again. I even added a little color to my wardrobe. I now have daily affirmations that pop up on my phone every morning to remind me of how beautiful I truly am, no matter what size I am. I love me and who I am. I am glad for what I went through growing up because it made me into the confident woman that I am today. I am back to being that little girl who stays in the mirror admiring who she is. I love me, and I love my body. Every back roll, stretch mark, cellulite and fupa. It belongs to me and I love it. I am happy with who I am. This is me, and your opinion of me does not define who I am . One take away that I have from this journey is that it is important to love yourself from the inside and out including mind, body and soul.

ABOUT THE AUTHOR:

Social Media:

IG @pretty.broke_and_fierce

Email yendi.jones84@gmail.com

Yendi Jones is a beautiful young entrepreneur originally from New Jersey that now stays in the Pennsylvania area where she is the owner of her own dog grooming business, Pretty, Fluffy & Fierce. When she is not working at her full-time job or grooming dogs, you will find her spending time with her two fur babies Romeo and Nezuko or living her best life at Target. She is also a volunteer with the Girl Scouts, and has been a troop leader for four years which she truly enjoys doing. Yendi is currently the co-host of Positive isn't Popular podcast which you can listen to every Tuesday.

ABOUT THE LEAD AUTHOR

Kenneth Wilson is a native of Silver Spring, MD. He is the Founder and CEO of Men of Stature and Black Squirrel Media. He has professional experience in business, education, politics, and public safety. He is also a passionate community advocate who has worked with people globally.

As a consultant, he has worked with businesses, non-profit organizations, churches, and political outfits all over the world. He has developed programs that have helped dozens of aspiring entrepreneurs begin and pursue their business dreams.

He also has a passion to be a voice in the community, which includes hosting several podcasts and virtual shows. Kenneth can be heard weekly as Co-Host of the Community Coalition Show, Reason & Rhyme Podcast, and The Speakeasy Show.

As a public speaker, he discusses issues involving the Black community, with a focus on Black men. He also discusses and teaches seminars on business development. In the field of safety, he is a certified CPR/First Aid Instructor. He teaches courses in person and virtually.

Accomplishments
- 2016 President's Lifetime Achievement Award Winner
- Two-time Bestselling Author
- Founder and CEO of Black Squirrel Media & Men of Stature
- Creator of the B.LIT Festival & Black Squirrel Media Network
- International Safety Expert and Community Advocate

Social Media:
IG @mrkennethwilson
FB @mrkennethwilson
LinkedIn: @kennywilson65
Email kennywilson65@gmail.com

PICK UP THESE OTHER TITLES BY KENNETH WILSON

 BLACK MEN LOVE

 SUITED FOR SUCCESS: VOLUME 2

 THE IMPACT OF INFLUENCE: VOLUME 2

 **THE WINNING MINDSET**

 CONCRETE CONNECTION

To order your autographed copies visit

www.kennethrwilson.com

WORK WITH KENNETH

SPEAKING
LET ME HELP YOUR COMPANY, ORGANIZATION, OR COMMUNITY GROUP LEARN THE VALUE OF BUILDING LASTING RELATIONSHIPS.

TRAINING
LEARN EMERGENCY PREPAREDNESS AND LIFE-SAVING TECHNIQUES FOR THE WORKPLACE AND THE COMMUNITY.

COMMUNITY BUILDING
CONNECT WITH SAFE SPACES AND INITIATIVES SPECIFIC TO BLACK MEN AND THE BLACK COMMUNITY.

KENNETHRWILSON.COM

Made in the USA
Middletown, DE
28 February 2023

25852054R00070